BEHIND THE SCENES BIOGRAPHIES

WHAT YOU NEVER KNEW ABOUT

>>> ———— <<<

ZENDAYA

by Dr. Nafeesah Allen

CAPSTONE PRESS
a capstone imprint

This is an unauthorized biography.

Published by Spark, an imprint of Capstone
1710 Roe Crest Drive, North Mankato, Minnesota 56003
capstonepub.com

Library of Congress Cataloging-in-Publication Data
Names: Allen, Nafeesah, author.
Title: What you never knew about Zendaya / by Nafeesah Allen.
Description: North Mankato, Minnesota : Capstone Press, [2024] | Series: Behind the scenes biographies | Includes bibliographical references and index. | Audience: Ages 9 to 11 | Audience: Grades 4-6 | Summary: "Zendaya's star power is so bright, she only needs to go by one name. She can sing, she can dance, and she can act! But what is her life like when she's not performing? High-interest details and bold photos of her high-profile life will enthrall reluctant and struggling readers, while carefully levelled text will leave them feeling confident"— Provided by publisher.
Identifiers: LCCN 2022058784 (print) | LCCN 2022058785 (ebook) | ISBN 9781669049494 (hardcover) | ISBN 9781669049364 (paperback) | ISBN 9781669049371 (pdf) | ISBN 9781669049395 (kindle edition) | ISBN 9781669049401 (epub)
Subjects: LCSH: Zendaya, 1996- — Juvenile literature. | Actors—United States—Biography—Juvenile literature. | Singers—United States—Biography—Juvenile literature. | Models (Persons)—United States—Biography—Juvenile literature. | LCGFT: Biographies.
Classification: LCC PN2287.Z47 A49 2024 (print) | LCC PN2287.Z47 (ebook) | DDC 791.4302/8092 [B]—dc23/eng/20230119
LC record available at https://lccn.loc.gov/2022058784
LC ebook record available at https://lccn.loc.gov/2022058785

Editorial Credits
Editor: Mandy Robbins; Designer: Heidi Thompson; Media Researcher: Jo Miller; Production Specialist: Tori Abraham

Image Credits
Alamy: BFA, 21, Classic Image, 19, PictureLux / The Hollywood Archive, 28, Rolf Adlercreutz, 26, UPI, 23, 27; Associated Press: Chris Pizzello/Invision, 13 (bottom, top), 25, John Salangsang/Invision, 7; Getty Images: David Livingston, 17, Momodu Mansaray, Cover; Newscom: AXELLE/BAUER-GRIFFIN / MEGA, 20, Johns PKI / Splash News, 14; Shutterstock: BondRocketImages, 18, Color Symphony, 29 (brushes), cynoclub, 22, DFree, 4, 9, ipunk kristianto, 24, Irina Matsiash, 15, Jaguar PS, 10, margouillat photo, 8, mhatzapa, 11, 12, 13 (musical notes), Nadin Panina, 16 (bottom), onair, 16 (top), Thammasak Lek, 29 (watercolors), Tinseltown, 13 (middle)

All internet sites appearing in back matter were available and accurate when this book was sent to press.

Printed and bound in China. PO5379

TABLE OF CONTENTS

Words in **bold** are in the glossary.

A BUSY WOMAN

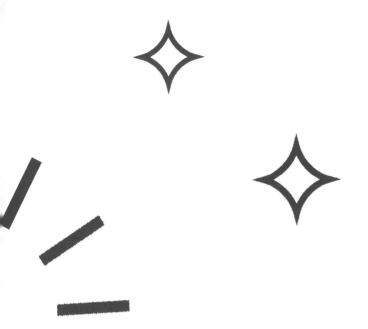

Zendaya is more than an actress and a singer. She's a dancer. She's a model. Z is even a **producer**, an author, and a fashion designer. She started her clothing line, Daya, at 20 years old.

What else might surprise you about Zendaya?

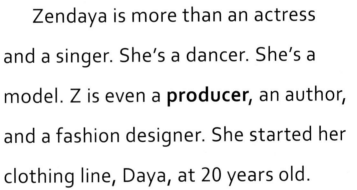

WHAT'S IN A
NAME?

Zendaya was born September 1, 1996.
Her dad loved the word "Zen." Her parents
combined it with the Shona word *tendai*.
It means "to offer thanks."

FACT
The Shona people are from
Zimbabwe and South Africa.

Zendaya and her parents

POP QUIZ!

Will you pass this Zendaya pop quiz?

1. **What's her favorite ice cream flavor?**

2. **Who calls her "M.J." in real life?**

3. **What's the hip-hop group she danced with in Oakland?**

4. **How many siblings does she have?**

1. Häagen-Dazs coffee   2. Tom Holland

3. Future Shock   4. Five—three sisters and two brothers

DANCING TO THE
MUSIC

Zendaya started dancing with Future Shock at eight years old. She danced back-up for Selena Gomez in a 2009 commercial. Z even took second place on *Dancing with the Stars* in 2013.

FACT

At only 16, Zendaya was the youngest person yet to be on *Dancing with the Stars*.

Zendaya has been in music videos with Bruno Mars, Taylor Swift, and Beyoncé! She makes music videos for her own songs too. They include "Replay" and "Neverland."

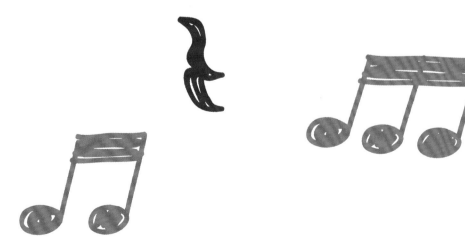

Bruno Mars

Taylor Swift

Beyoncé

A (ROLE) MODEL

Zendaya has modeled for Old Navy, Macy's, and Valentino. She tries to be a role model too. In 2013, she released her book *Between U and Me*. In it, she gives young people advice on growing up and chasing their dreams. She also talks about having good relationships. She encourages kids to have their own personal style.

Zendaya often does her own makeup for events. That included the 2022 Oscars. But a big part of her beauty **routine** is skincare. She wears sunscreen every day. And she always takes her makeup off before bed.

BORN INTO THE ARTS

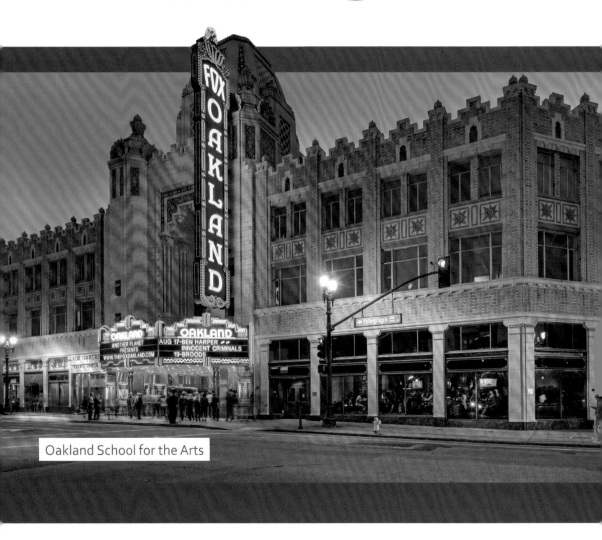

Oakland School for the Arts

Zendaya learned about acting when she was little. Her mother worked at the Shakespeare Theatre in Orinda, California. Zendaya went to Oakland School for the Arts. There, she learned to act and dance. Z's first acting role was in the Shakespeare play, *Macbeth*.

FACT
Both of Zendaya's parents are teachers. If Zendaya weren't acting, she thinks she would be too.

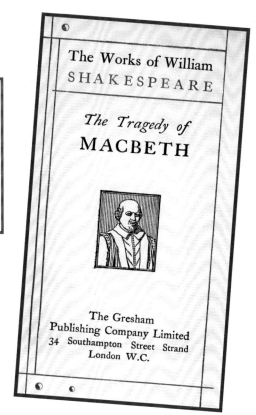

The Works of William
SHAKESPEARE

The Tragedy of
MACBETH

The Gresham
Publishing Company Limited
34 Southampton Street Strand
London W.C.

ZENDAYA'S LOVES

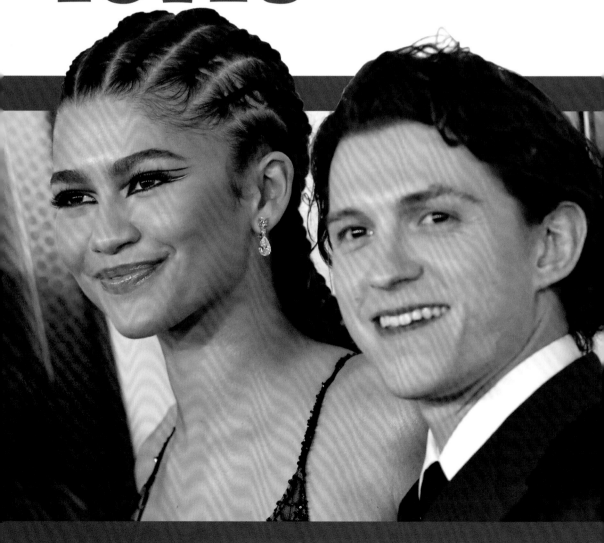

It's no secret that Zendaya is dating Tom Holland. They made it public in 2021. The pair met filming *Spider-Man—No Way Home* in 2016. Even crazier, on Z's first date she went to an earlier Spider-Man movie. (That date wasn't with Tom.)

Who else stole Z's heart? Her dog, Noon. His Instagram account has almost 30,000 followers.

Who's her celebrity crush? Channing Tatum. Why? She loves his dance moves. They worked together on the film *Smallfoot*.

Common, Zendaya, and Channing Tatum

JUSTICE
WARRIOR

When she was 16, Zendaya pushed Disney to cast a black family in her series *K.C. Undercover.* Zendaya starred as a spy trained in **martial arts**. Want a laugh? Her character was bad at dancing and singing.

During the 2015 Oscars, someone made a **racist** comment about Z's hair on *E!'s Fashion Police*. The next day, Zendaya responded on Instagram.

"My wearing my hair in locs . . . was to showcase them in a positive light, to remind people of color that our hair is good enough."

-Zendaya, Instagram, February 23, 2015

BRUSH IT OFF

Z works hard! How does she chill? She paints watercolors! Her *Euphoria* co-star Hunter Schafer got her an art book. She says that painting helps her to become less controlling.

Glossary

martial arts (MAR-shuhl ARTS)—styles of self-defense and fighting; tae kwon do, judo, and karate are examples of martial arts

producer (pruh-DOOS-ur)—the person in charge of making a TV show or movie

racist (RAY-sist)—prejudice or discrimination against a person or group of a different race based on negative beliefs about that race

routine (roo-TEEN)—a set of moves done in a set order

sibling (SIB-ling)—one of two or more individuals having the same parents or sometimes only one parent in common

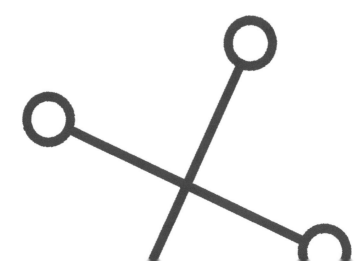

Read More

Anderson, Kirsten. *Who Is Zendaya?* New York: Penguin Workshop, 2022.

Johnson, Robin. *Zendaya*. New York: Crabtree Publishing Company, 2018.

Schwartz, Heather E. *Zendaya: Hollywood Superstar.* Minneapolis: Lerner Publications, 2023.

Internet Sites

Want to Know Every Single Fact About Zendaya? Same, Let's Go
cosmopolitan.com/entertainment/celebs/a32928868/zendaya-facts/

Zendaya
zendaya.com

Zendaya: Instagram
instagram.com/zendaya/?hl=en

Index

About the Author

Dr. Nafeesah Allen is a world traveler, wife, and mom. Her family speaks English, Spanish, and Portuguese, and loves good music. Her favorite activity is to host surprise dance parties in her kitchen.